A Fun Guide just ~~for girls~~ ages 6-9

Just For Me!
My Family

Katrina Cassel

LEGACY PRESS®
www.LegacyPressKids.com

Family book dedication:

Rick: Best friend and guide

Tyler: Firstborn

Jessica: Firstborn princess

Jeff: My determined one

Adam: Warrior in the making

Jasmine: My joy and song

Kaleb and Kayla: Chosen ones

And to the others who have been a part of our family whether for a few days or a few months. God has a special plan for each of you.

A special thanks to the Legacy team who brings each book to life and to Teresa for all her suggestions.

JUST FOR ME: MY FAMILY
©2010 by Legacy Press
ISBN 10: 1-58411-095-3
ISBN 13: 978-1-58411-095-8
Legacy reorder#: LP48413
JUVENILE NONFICTION / Religion / Christianity / Christian Life

Legacy Press
P.O. Box 261129
San Diego, CA 92196
www.LegacyPressKids.com

Mixed Sources
Product group from well-managed forests and other controlled sources
www.fsc.org   Cert no. GFA-COC-001990
©1996 Forest Stewardship Council

FSC

Cover Illustrator: Dave Carleson
Interior Illustrator: Shelley Dieterichs

Scriptures are from the *Holy Bible: New International Version* (North American Edition), ©1973, 1978, 1984 by the International Bible Society. Used by permission of Zondervan Bible Publishers.

Printed in the United States of America

Hi Girlfriend!

Welcome to Just for Me: My Family!

Families are important and this book will be your guide to learning more about your own family. In this book you will:

❋ Learn about the first family.

❋ Find out why God made families.

❋ Learn more about your parents.

❋ Find out how to get along better with your siblings.

❋ Find ways to work together as a family.

❋ Discover new ideas for family fun.

❋ Discover ideas for serving together.

❋ Learn fun facts about animal families.

Each chapter of Just for Me: My Family is full of fun facts, clever ideas, crafts, and family games. You'll find verses, stories, puzzles, and more. So hurry inside and get started—and don't forget to invite your family along!

Table of Contents

God Made Families

Ava skipped up the steps to her house and opened the door. She hung her backpack and jacket on her special hook.

"How was school?" Mom asked. She was in the kitchen giving Ava's three-year-old sister, Hannah, a snack.

"It was okay. We're talking about families in social studies. Our assignment for tonight is to think about how families began and why they are important." Ava took an apple slice from the plate.

"You just have to look in the first two chapters of Genesis to find out how families began." Mom wiped Hannah's face and let her out of her booster seat.

Ava went to her room and found her children's Bible storybook and began to read.

The First Family

Trees

Clouds

Birds

Flowers

Sea

Man

Sky

Fish

Woman

Stars

Plants

Children

Long ago there was no world. There were no

or , or . There was only God. God

decided to create a beautiful world. He made the

and put in it. He made the and filled it

with . God made land and covered it with ,

9

and . He made to fly in the

and all kinds of animals to roam the land.

Then, God made a and named him Adam. God

brought all the animals that He'd created to Adam to be

named. Adam must have had fun thinking up all the

different animal names! God didn't want Adam to be

lonely, so He created a . Her name was Eve.

Adam and Eve were the first husband and wife. Now

Adam had someone to talk to. He had a best friend. Soon

Adam and Eve had sons. First they had Cain, then Abel,

and then Seth. They had more later. Adam and

Eve's family was the start of all the families in the world.

Q: What was one of Adam's jobs?

_____

Q: Why did God create Eve?

_____

The Purpose of Families

"I think we have families so we won't be alone," Ava said thoughtfully. "That's why God created Eve—so Adam wouldn't get lonely, and so Adam and Eve could have children and be the first family."

"That's right," Mom said. "Families were God's idea. He wanted people to belong together. You, Dad, Hannah, and I are a family. We each have our own place in the family."

Ava sat down to play with Hannah. She stacked up colorful wooden blocks to make a tower. "Dad goes to work everyday. He makes sure we have money for things we need. You take care of us, and I help with Hannah after school. I also do the dishes after supper every night."

"That's true. But Dad does more than just go to work to make money. Can you think of some other things he does?" Mom asked.

"That's easy," Ava said. "He practices soccer with me. He takes Hannah and me to the park. He helps me with homework, too."

"There are things each of us do in our family. Each person is important." Mom added a red block to the top of the tower.

"I'm glad that God thought of families," Ava said. "Everyone should have a family to love them and care for them."

Can you list three ways your parents care for you?

1. _____

2. _____

3. _____

Puzzle Pieces Family Puzzle Verse

Below is a verse that tells us something about families. Each flower below has a number and letter in it. There is also a number under each line. Look at the number below the first line. Find the flower with that number. Write the letter in the flower on the line. Continue doing that until you can read the whole verse. *Puzzle answers appear at the back of the book.*

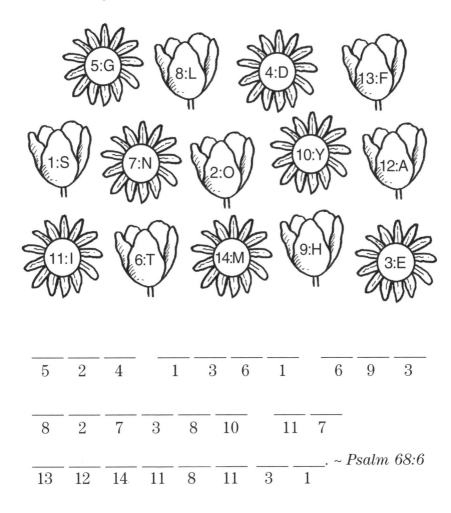

5:G   8:L   4:D   13:F

1:S   7:N   2:O   10:Y   12:A

11:I   6:T   14:M   9:H   3:E

___ ___ ___   ___ ___ ___ ___   ___ ___ ___
 5   2   4   1   3   6   1   6   9   3

___ ___ ___ ___ ___ ___   ___ ___
 8   2   7   3   8   10   11   7

___ ___ ___ ___ ___ ___ ___ ___. ~ *Psalm 68:6*
13   12   14   11   8   11   3   1

God's plan is for families to live together, and to take care of each other. God doesn't want people to be lonely!

Animal Families: Koala Joeys!

Children aren't the only ones that need families to care for them. Animal babies need parents to care for them too! Have you ever seen a cuddly koala at the zoo? It may look like a fuzzy bear, but it's not a bear at all. It's part of a group of animals that carry their babies in pouches. They are called *marsupials*.

When a koala is born, it is about the size of a large jellybean. It's not ready to be out in the world yet. The newborn koala, called a *joey*, is born without fur. It can't see or hear at first, but it can climb. The first thing it does after it's born is to climb into its mother's pouch. It stays there for six months just eating, sleeping, and growing. The joey grows fur during that time.

After six months, it starts wandering out, but it still returns to its mother's pouch to sleep and to hide from danger.

After the *joey* outgrows the pouch, it climbs onto its mother's back and hangs on with specially created hands and feet, which have claws. The hands have two thumbs to make it easier to hold on when the ride gets bumpy. Specially ridged skin on the feet gives the koala good traction. The ridged skin keeps the koala from sliding when it climbs. The koala has strong arm and shoulder muscles for climbing. When it is about a year old, the koala can live alone in the trees.

▶ How does the mother koala protect her baby?

_____

_____

_____

▶ Can you think of two ways your parents protect you?

1.

_____

2.

_____

Family Tree

It's fun to make a family tree so you can see where you came from! Here is a family tree you can make for you and your family.

 ## You Will Need:

 Poster board in your favorite color

 Green paper or craft foam

 Brown paper or craft foam

 Red paper or craft foam

 Marker

Photos or names of family members—you can include just the family living in your house or add extended family as well (grandparents, aunts and uncles, cousins, etc.).

 Scissors

 Glue

 ## Do This:

✳ From the green paper or foam, cut a large oval shape to be the top of the tree. It can be as large as you want.

Using the brown paper or foam, cut a tree trunk the correct size for the treetop you made.

 Glue the treetop and bottom on the poster board.

 Write your name on the tree trunk.

 Cut a red apple shape (or shape of your choice) for each family member.

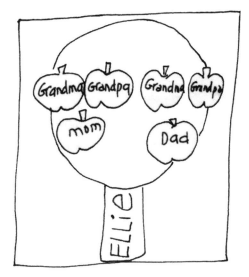

 Write a family member's name or put a picture on each apple.

 Place your mom's and dad's names on opposite sides of the tree.

 Glue the apples on the tree.

 Put their parents' names above them. If you are including your aunts and uncles, put their names next to your mom's or dad's name. Your parents can help you with this.

 Hang your family tree where you can see it.

Family Time

Ava entered the house and found her mom doing the laundry. She was very excited.

"Guess what? I did great in social studies today. I shared with the class how families were God's idea, and how God created Eve so that Adam wouldn't be alone," Ava said.

"That's great," Mom said folding a shirt. "Tell me about it."

"Everyone got a chance to tell about his or her family. I shared some things that you and Dad do for us. Other students talked about what their families like to do together, too," Ava said as she helped her mom fold socks.

"Speaking of what families do together, what would you like to do tonight for family time?" Mom asked.

"Can we play our indoor bowling game?" Ava said. "Even Hannah can play that."

"Okay." Mom handed Ava her pile of clean clothes. "You put these away and then get what we need for the game. We'll have everything ready by the time Dad gets home."

"Okay." Ava took her clothes and put them neatly in her drawers.

Ava's Indoor Bowling Game

Want to play Ava's indoor bowling game with your family?

You Will Need:

- 20 plastic disposable cups in your favorite color
- Sand or play dough (to weigh down the cups)
- Tape
- Tennis ball or other small ball

Do This:

- Set ten cups upright
- Press a ball of play dough or pour 1 inch of sand in each cup.
- Place a cup upside down on top of the upright cup.
- Tape where the two cups come together. Tape thoroughly so that sand doesn't leak out.

✽ Arrange the cups in bowling pin fashion—one in the first row, two in the second row, three in the third row, and four in the fourth row.

✽ The first player moves back from the pins, rolls the ball and tries to knock down as many cups as they can. They have two tries to knock down the cups.

✽ Reset the cups, and repeat with each new player.

✽ Play until someone knocks down at least 30 cups. Then begin a new game.

Y ou've read about the first family and you've learned a little about what families do for each other, including the koala mother and baby. There's more fun ahead!

Part of the Family

Abby and Ashley sat together in their third grade church class. The lesson today was about Bible families.

"I want each person to share a little about their own family. Tell how many brothers and sisters you have and how old they are," Mrs. Evans said. "Then, I'm going to tell you a story about a Bible family."

Ella talked about her two younger brothers. Then, Tamika shared how she and her two older sisters were adopted from Haiti. Finally, it was Abby and Ashley's turn.

"Ashley and I are twins." Abby smiled at her sister.

"But I'm older by twelve minutes," Ashley said.

"Tell us about the rest of your family," Mrs. Evans said.

"We have an older brother, Jacob, who is twelve," Abby said.

"And he is super bossy," Ashley added, making a face. The other girls laughed.

"That's because he's the oldest," Abby explained. "And we have a younger brother named Michael. He's four."

After everyone had shared about his or her family,

Mrs. Evans got out her big Bible story cards. "Today we're going to talk about Moses' family," she said.

Moses' Family

Baby Moses   River

Basket   Miriam

Moses' mother and father were Israelites who lived in Egypt. The wicked Pharaoh (the King of Egypt) didn't like the Israelites living in his country, so he forced the Israelites to be his slaves. He decided to kill all the baby boys so they couldn't grow up and fight against him.

Jochebed, ☺ ' mother, loved ☺ very much. She didn't want the Pharaoh's men to kill him so she hid ☺ in the house for three months. When ☺

was too big to hide in the house, she decided to hide

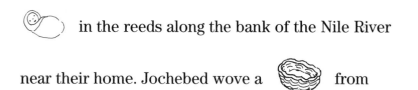 in the reeds along the bank of the Nile River

near their home. Jochebed wove a 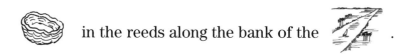 from

papyrus reeds. She coated the outside with tar and pitch

so that it would float. Then, she put inside the

 in the reeds along the bank of the .

"Stay hidden and keep an eye on baby Moses,"

Jochebed told Moses' sister, .

Pharaoh's daughter went to the to bathe.

She saw the among the reeds and sent her

maid to get it. The princess peeked into the basket and

saw . The princess knew he was an Israelite

baby. She knew about her father's cruel order to kill all

the baby boys.

"I will keep him for myself," she told her maid.

 ran out from her hiding place. "Would you

like me to find someone to care for the baby until he is

old enough to live with you?" she asked the princess.

Moses' own mother cared for until he was

old enough to live at the palace. Then, she took him to

the princess who raised Moses as her own son. God had

plans for Moses, and this was just the beginning.

Mrs. Evans put the Bible story away. "That's all for

today," she said. "Next week we will talk more about

Bible families."

> **Q:** Why did Moses' mother put him in a

basket along the river?_____

> **Q:** What was Miriam's job?

Families Take Care of Each Other

Your mother didn't hide you in a basket but she did care for you. She fed you and changed your diapers. Your dad probably helped with that, too. He may have taught you to ride a bike or to throw a ball. Your mom and dad cook and clean, buy groceries, and repair things that break. Maybe you have an older brother or sister who helps do some of those things too. You may have your own special job to do in your family such as emptying the wastebaskets or dusting. **Each family member plays a special part in the family.**

List three things each family member does to help care for each other.

Dad

1. _____
2. _____
3. _____

Mom

1. _____
2. _____
3. _____

Sisters or brothers

1. _____

2. _____

3. _____

Animal Friends

Animal Families: Penguin Chicks!

Millions of Emperor Penguins live in the frozen Antarctic. The male Emperor penguin should win the "Dad of the Year" award for his care of his unborn chick. After the mom penguin lays an egg, the dad penguin immediately takes the egg and cradles it on top of his feet. The blood vessels in his feet are specially made to keep his feet from getting cold. Loose layers of skin lay over top of the egg, keeping the egg warm. The dad penguin balances the egg that way for two months.

To keep warm during this long process, penguin dads huddle together, hardly moving. They face inward, with their backs to the cold. During this time, the dads don't eat. They live on body fat they have stored up ahead of time.

Once the penguin chick is hatched, it stays on its dad's feet until the mother returns from fishing in the sea. The mother then takes over parenting so the dad penguin can finally eat!

The Emperor Penguin is the largest penguin.
How do you compare?

Emperor Penguin: Me:

Around 45 inches tall   _____ inches tall

Weighs 40-100 pounds   I weigh _____ pounds

Are you taller or shorter than the penguin? _____

Do you weigh more or less than a penguin? _____

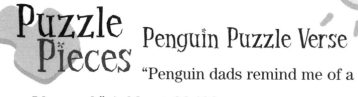

Puzzle Pieces   Penguin Puzzle Verse

"Penguin dads remind me of a verse I learned," Ashley told Abby.

If you decode the puzzle below, you can read the verse Ashley was thinking about. Look at the number in each penguin egg. Write that word on the line that has that same number. *Puzzle answers appear at the back of the book.*

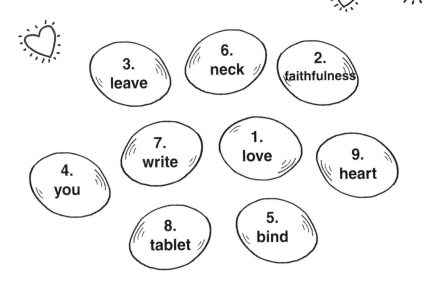

Let _____ and _____ never _____
　　　1　　　　　　　　　　2　　　　　　　　　　3

_____;　_____ them around
　　　　4　　　　　　　　5

your _____,　_____ them on the _____
　　　　　6　　　　　　7　　　　　　　　　　8

of your _____.　~ *Proverbs 3:3*
　　　　　9.

What two things should be written on your heart? Write them in the heart below.

Penguin Cupcakes

Here are cupcakes you can make to remind you of penguins and how they care for their children.

The directions that follow show how to make a cupcake that resembles a Macaroni Penguin, a species with colorful markings. The Macaroni Penguin has orange eyebrow feathers that stick out from a small patch on his forehead and a sturdy red bill. Macaroni penguins are about 28 inches tall and weigh nine pounds. Both the mom and dad penguin help keep the egg warm before the chick is hatched.

If you would rather make an Emperor Penguin, just leave off the eyebrow feathers and add black around the sides of the cupcake.

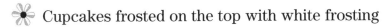

 ## You Will Need:

- Cupcakes frosted on the top with white frosting
- Red and black jellybeans
- Chocolate graham cracker (cookie) sticks
- Orange or yellow licorice
- Red Fruit Roll-Ups®
- Clean kitchen scissors

You may substitute other kinds of candy or even fruit to make this penguin

 ## Do This:

- Cut penguin feet from the Fruit Roll-Up and place them so that they hang off of the bottom of the cupcake.
- Put one graham cracker stick on each side of the

cupcake sticking out to the side for wings.

✳ Place a red jellybean in the middle for the bill. You may cut the jellybean in half length-wise for a smaller bill.

✳ Cut a black jellybean in half cross-wise. Use a half for each eye.

✳ Cut thin pieces of an orange or yellow licorice for eyebrow feathers. Place them at the outside corner of the eyes, fanning upward.

✳ Your penguin is done! Make one for each family member or to share with your classmates.

• • • • • • • • • • • • • • • • • • • •

Abby and Ashley finished making their cupcakes. "Wow," Ashley said. "I love the wild orange feathers."

"Me too. May we take penguin cupcakes to school for our birthday next week?" Abby asked her mom.

"Yes, may we?" Ashley asked. "We are studying them in our animal unit in science class."

"Okay," Mom agreed. "If you help make them."

"We'll make half the cupcakes to look like Macaroni Penguins and half to look like Emperor Penguins," Ashley said. "I think it's great how the dad Emperor Penguin takes care of the egg."

"I know a game we can play to pretend we are penguins," Abby said. "Want to play?"

"Sure," Ashley said. "Just tell me how."

Want to play Abby's penguin game? Just follow the directions below. It's easy and your whole family can play.

Protect the Egg Game

 You Will Need:

✱ One large-sized plastic Easter egg filled with sand or a ball of clay (to make the egg heavier) for each family member. You will want to tape the eggs shut if you use sand. Hacky sack type balls or beanbags will also work.

Do This:

❋ Have all the players stand side by side with their "eggs" balanced on their feet.

❋ On the signal, players must walk across the room without losing their egg or letting it touch the ground. The egg must touch both feet at all times.

❋ If you drop your egg, you're out. Use a shuffling motion so that you don't lose your egg.

❋ The first one across the room while keeping their egg safe wins.

In the first two chapters, you learned ways that families care for each other. In the next chapter, you will learn some things that make families special. Read on—there are more games, crafts and fun things to do ahead!

Chapter 3

My Family is Special

Higher," Sarah yelled. Sarah and her sisters, Lauren and Natalie, were flying kites on the beach with their dad. He was helping Sarah unroll her kite string to make her kite fly high into the sky.

"Look at mine," Natalie said as she let out more string. "It's so high it looks like a bird."

"Look, look," Lauren called. "Mine high."

"It sure is," Sarah said. Lauren had a toddler-sized kite that was barely off of the sand, but Sarah remembered having a kite like Lauren's when she was that age.

"Fly *your* kite, Dad," said Natalie.

Dad had a special kite that had two strings instead

of one so he could make it do tricks. First he made it do a loop, then double loops. The kite soared, then dipped.

"Let me try it," Sarah said as she reached for the kite.

"Okay, I'll show you what to do," Dad said.

It was harder than it looked! Several times the kite almost crashed. Finally, Sarah could make the kite turn a loop with Dad's help.

"It's almost lunch time," Dad said. "We'd better get home."

"Hungry!" Lauren said.

Mom was making lunch when Dad and the three girls arrived home.

"Tell us a story while we wait for lunch," Natalie said.

"Okay." Dad sat on the couch. "What story?"

"How about the story of Abraham and Sarah?" Natalie sat down next to him.

"I will if you help me tell it," Dad said.

Abraham and Sarah

Abraham   Sarah   Baby

Dad began to tell Sarah, Natalie and Lauren the

story of and .

" and loved God. They did everything

37

that God asked them to do. But they were sad." Dad

looked at Natalie.

"They were sad because they didn't have any children

of their own," Natalie said.

"God promised that his family would be great,

which meant large in numbers. asked how that

could be when he didn't have any children," Dad said.

"The stars, the stars," Lauren said, bouncing up and

down on the couch.

"That's right, Lauren." Dad sat her on his lap. "God

told to go outside and count the stars if he could."

"But he couldn't. No one can count all the stars

because there are so many. God told that his family

would be like the number of stars," Sarah said.

"God told him that would have a ,"

Natalie said.

"Isaac. Call him Isaac," Lauren said. She slid off Dad's

lap and spun in a circle. She tumbled over.

Dad laughed and put her back on his lap. "That's right,

Lauren. They would have a and would name him

Isaac. But laughed because she didn't believe that

she would really have a child in her old age."

"God asked why she had laughed," Natalie

said. "Sarah was afraid because she had laughed, so she

lied and said she hadn't laughed."

"God kept His promise and had a just

as God said." Sarah sat back, the story over.

Just as they finished the story, Mom came into the

room to tell them it was time to eat lunch.

 **Q:** What did God promise Abraham?

_____

_____

 Q: Why did Sarah laugh?

_____

Families are Special

One reason that families are special is because of the things that they do for each other. Here are five things that families do for each other:

1. Love each other
2. Talk and listen to each other
3. Work as a team
4. Care about each other
5. Share fun times

Love Each Other

There are many ways families show that they love each other. One way your parents show you that they love you is by providing you with the things you need.

Can you think of two things you need that your family provides? List them here:

1. _____

2. _____

Talk and Listen to Each Other

Do you take time to talk to your mom, dad and siblings? Do you take time to listen when other family members talk? Read on to learn what Sarah and her family do as they eat dinner:

"It's my turn to pick the question," Sarah said as soon as the blessing was said. She reached into the basket and pulled out a folded up slip of paper. She opened it and read, "If you could go anywhere on vacation, where would you go?"

Sarah thought for a minute. "I'd go to Japan to see the cherry blossoms we read about in social studies."

"I'd go to Africa to see all the animals," Natalie said.

Mom, Dad and even Lauren gave their answers, too.

"Tomorrow it will be Natalie's turn to pick the question," Mom said.

✳ Just for Me! ✳

You can do the same thing at a meal as Sarah and her family. Just have everyone think of questions and write them on slips of paper. Fold them up and put them in a basket or other container. Pick one out of the basket each day. Everyone gets a turn to answer the question.

What are two questions you could ask your family? Write them here.

➤ 1. _____

➤ 2. _____

Work as a Team

"Come girls," Dad said. "It's Saturday and we're cleaning the garage today."

"Me help," Lauren said.

"Okay, Lauren," Dad said. "You and Natalie can take the newspapers and cans to the curb for recycling."

"What can I do to help?" Sarah asked.

"You, Mom, and I will take everything out of the garage. Then you can sweep while Mom and I sort through things and decide what to keep and what to get rid of." Dad picked up a box and carried it to the driveway.

Everyone worked hard and soon there were piles of things to be recycled. There were bags to go to the thrift shop and bags to go out with the trash. Sarah swept the garage floor. The garage looked clean and tidy.

"Great job. Everyone worked together and the job is done. Now it's time to have fun," Dad said.

"Yippee," the girls said.

Does your family work together to get things done? Working may not be as much fun as playing, but it is part of being a family. What is one job that you can help with at home? Write it down here:

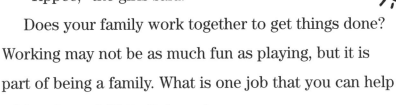

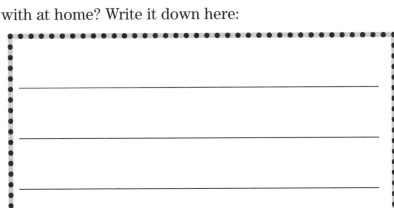

Puzzle Pieces   Care About Each Other Kite Puzzle Verse

Families care about each other. You can read what the Bible says about the way people should treat each other. Simply decode the verses below by looking at the number under each line. Find the kite with that number and write the word on the line. *Puzzle answers appear at the back of the book.*

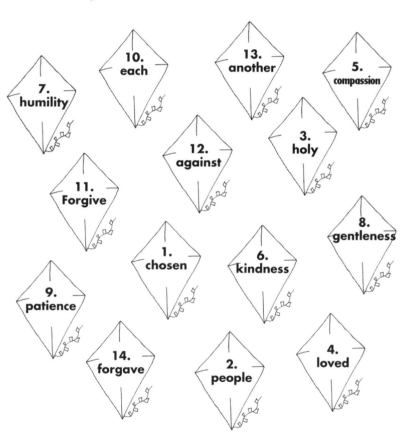

My Family is Special

Therefore, as God's _____ _____,
                        1   2

_____ and dearly _____,
      3   4

clothe yourselves with _____, _____,
                              5   6

_____, _____ and _____.
      7   8   9

Bear with _____ other and _____whatever
              10   11

grievances you may have _____ one _____.
                              12   13

_____ as the Lord _____ you.
      11   14

~ *Colossians 3:12-13*

45

Animal Families: Owl Chicks!

When the mom and dad owl first meet, they are afraid of each other. This is natural for owls. It keeps them safe. If the dad owl wants the mom owl's attention, he may drop a gift of food for her nearby.

Mom and dad owls have between two and six chicks at one time. The mom takes good care of the owl chicks. She feeds them, protects them from other animals, and teaches them how to fly. Soon they leave the nest and find

their own places to live. The father helps by sitting on the eggs before they hatch and providing food for the family.

Does this sound at all like your family? Your mom and dad provide food for you and teach you the things you will need to know to live on your own one day. It just takes a lot longer for children to grow up than it does for owl chicks!

Magnetic Owl

This craft will remind you that families are special and that families take care of each other.

 ## You Will Need:

- 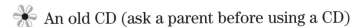 An old CD (ask a parent before using a CD)
- Tan craft foam or felt
- Light brown craft foam or felt
- Dark brown craft foam or felt
- Wiggle eyes
- Magnet strip or small round magnet
- Scissors
- Glue

 ## Do This:

Trace the circle and two ears on light brown craft foam or felt.

Trace the heart shape on tan craft foam or felt.

✳ Just for Me! ✳

✳ Trace the nose (triangle) on dark brown craft foam or felt.

✳ Glue the light brown circle to the CD.

✳ Glue the heart on top of the circle.

✳ Glue the ears—one at the top of each side of the heart.

✳ Glue the nose in the middle with the triangle pointing down.

✳ Glue on the wiggle eyes.

✳ Glue or stick the magnet to the back.

✳ Allow to dry, then hang on your refrigerator to remind you that families are special.

You can substitute colors to make your owl unique.

Sarah, Lauren, and Natalie enjoy spending time together as a family. Sometimes they play miniature golf and get ice cream. Other times, they fly kites on the beach or in the park. One of their favorite things to do is play games. They like to play tic-tac-toe and they have two different ways to play it. One way is outside on the sidewalk and another way is inside with pieces they can eat! You can find out how to play both ways below.

Tic-Tac-Toe Games

If it's a nice day outside, you can play tic-tac-toe outside. All you need is a flat place to play (like a driveway or sidewalk), chalk, pennies, and nickels.

  # Outside:

* Draw a big tic-tac-toe grid.

* Player One throws a penny and tries to land it in a square.

* Player Two throws a nickel and tries to land it in a square.

❋ If the coin misses the grid, it doesn't count and it is the next player's turn.

❋ If the coin lands in the same square as another coin, the player can try again.

❋ Continue to play the game just as you would on paper.

❋ The first player with three coins in a row wins.

Inside:

If it's a rainy day, you can play inside with edible pieces.

 ## You Will Need:

❋ Licorice pieces or red twists

❋ Gummy bears or candies in two different colors

 ## Do This:

 Place two pieces of licorice parallel on a plate. Place two pieces of licorice across the other two to form a tic-tac-toe grid.

50

❋ Player one chooses a candy color and places her piece on the grid.

❋ Player two uses another color and places her piece on the grid.

❋ Continue as you would in a regular tic-tac-toe game.

❋ When you are done, you can eat the board!

In this chapter you saw how families love each other, talk and listen to each other, work as a team, care about each other, and share fun times. You learned how owls are afraid of each other at first, but then become a family. And you learned how to make a yummy tic-tac-toe game. There's more fun ahead. Hurry on to the next chapter!

❀ Chapter 4 ❀

My Parents

Emily and Cody sat in the back seat of the car. They were traveling to an amusement park several hours from home and were almost there.

"I can't wait until we get to the amusement park." Emily circled a word in her word search puzzle. "I want to go on the Ferris wheel first."

"Not me," Cody said. "I don't like heights. I'd rather go on a roller coaster."

"Some of them go really high," Emily said.

"But the roller coaster is going so fast that I don't notice." Cody pulled a juice box from the cooler and opened it.

"Will you go on the Ferris wheel with me Mom?" Emily asked.

"I'm afraid I'm like Cody. I don't care for heights, but

I love roller coasters. The faster the better."

Emily giggled. "That's funny. I never knew you were wild at heart."

"Wild at heart as long as I'm not on a

Ferris wheel," Mom said. I think we'll all learn a lot about each other today. And before we get there, why don't you read to us from your Bible Cody?"

"Okay. I'll read about Jesus' parents, Mary and Joseph," said Cody.

Jesus' Parents

Mary   Joseph   Angel

Stable   Manger

God decided to send His son Jesus to earth as a baby.

God wanted very special parents to raise Jesus. God

chose [Mary] and [Joseph] for the job.

One day an angel appeared to [Mary] and told her not to

be afraid. He had wonderful news for her. She was going

to have a baby and would name Him Jesus. Jesus would

save people from their sins. The 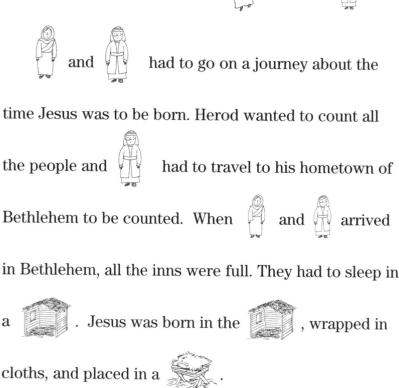 talked to too.

and had to go on a journey about the

time Jesus was to be born. Herod wanted to count all

the people and had to travel to his hometown of

Bethlehem to be counted. When and arrived

in Bethlehem, all the inns were full. They had to sleep in

a . Jesus was born in the , wrapped in

cloths, and placed in a .

Jesus grew up in the village of Nazareth in Israel. He

learned to walk and talk just like other children. He

learned to read and write and learned the Scriptures.

Jesus' earthly father was a carpenter. He taught

Jesus how to make things with wood.

When Jesus was twelve, and took him

to the temple in Jerusalem. He talked with important

men at the temple. The men were surprised at how

much Jesus knew about God and the Scriptures.

 and took good care of Jesus. They fed

him and taught him. They told him about the angel who

talked to them before He was born. Jesus loved

and and He loved His Heavenly Father, too.

"I'm glad that and took good care

of Jesus when He was a child," Cody said.

"I am, too," Dad said. "Mom and I try to take good

care of you just like and took care of Jesus."

Cody ended the story just as they pulled into the parking

lot. "Look, there's the amusement park, said Emily!"

▶ **Q:** How do you think Mary and Joseph felt when the angel told them they would be Jesus' earthly parents? _____

▶ **Q:** What things did they do to take care of Jesus?

Animal Families: Polar Bear Cubs!

Brrr. The wind is blowing and the temperature is below zero. Everything is frozen. Does this sound like a place you want to be? Probably not. Only a few animals can survive in a cold and lonely place like the Arctic.

You were probably born in a nice cozy hospital, but polar bear cubs are born in a den that the mother digs in the snow. It's much warmer in the den, and the mother bear can sleep and wait for the babies to be born.

A mama polar bear gives birth to her cubs in the winter. They are hairless and blind at birth and weigh about one pound. They depend on their mother for warmth and food. By the time they are four months old, the cubs weigh around twenty pounds each.

Polar bears eat meat; their favorite food is seal meat. Because of the cold climate in which they live, polar bears have to be very clever hunters.

The cubs are taught to hunt, protect themselves, and dig dens. When they are about two years old, they leave home and go off on their own. Polar bear cubs are very different from human children who live at home for many years before being ready to leave!

Parent Puzzle Verse

Read the following message from God to children about their parents. Look at the letter under the first line. Write the letter that comes next in the alphabet on the line above it. Continue doing this until you can read the Bible verse. The first letter is done to help you. *Puzzle answers appear at the back of the book.*

C
___ ___ ___ ___ ___ ___ ___ ___ ,   ___ ___ ___ ___
B   g   h   k   c   q   d   m   n   a   d   x

                           a
___ ___ ___ ___   ___ ___ ___ ___ ___ ___ ___
x   n   t   q   o   z   q   d   m   s   r

___ ___   ___ ___ ___   ___ ___ ___ ___ ,
h   m   s   g   d   K   n   q   c

___ ___ ___   ___ ___ ___ ___   ___ ___ ___
e   n   q   s   g   h   r   h   r

___ ___ ___ ___ ___ .   ~ *Ephesians 6:1*
q   h   f   g   s

What Do Parents Do?

It's important to listen to your parents because God put them here to take care of you. They have many jobs. Here are four of those jobs:

1. Protect you
2. Give you what you need
3. Teach you right from wrong
4. Love you

 ## Protect you

Parents start protecting you from the minute you are born. They make sure you are in a safe crib or car seat and that you don't fall off the changing table. When you are older, they teach you not to talk to strangers or run into the road. Animal mothers, like the ones we've read  about, have to keep their babies safe from wild animals! Aren't you glad your mom and dad don't have that job? Sometimes parents make rules to keep you safe. What is one rule your family has to keep you safe?

_____

_____

Give you what you need

Your parents provide a place to live, a bed to sleep in, clothes to wear, and food to eat. They keep your house warm when it is cold out, and cool when it is hot outside. They also provide water, light, and electricity.

Polar bears get food for their families, too. They sometimes wait patiently for hours for a seal to come up through an air hole in the ice. The seal becomes lunch for the bear family.

Polar Bear Maze

Help the mother polar bear find her cub. Start with the mother and make your way through the maze to the cub.

Teach you right from wrong

Sometimes this is not fun, but it's important. You have to know the difference between right and wrong to grow in your faith and to be a good citizen. It makes you more fun to be around, too. When you do something wrong, your mom or dad may have consequences for you such as sitting in time-out or losing a privilege. When you do something right, you may earn rewards or extra privileges.

Can you think of a good choice you made this week? What happened? _____

_____

Can you think of a bad choice you made this week? What happened? _____

_____

 # Love you

Your parents love you. They show you that by protecting you, giving you what you need, and helping you learn to do what is right. There are other ways that they show their love for you, too. They may play your favorite game with you, watch a movie with you, or take you somewhere special.

Draw a picture below of one way your parents show you that they love you.

Polar Bear Bank

You can do this craft to remind you of how the polar bear mom cares for her cubs, and how your parents care for you.

You Will Need:

 A two-liter soda bottle

 White paint

 Paintbrush

 Wiggle eyes

 Pompom for nose

 Marker

 Cloth for scarf or sock for hat

 Do This:

 Rinse out the soda bottle and let it dry.

 Paint the bottle white. You may have to paint it a second and third time.

 Glue on wiggle eyes or draw on eyes and eyelashes.

 Draw the ears—one on each side of the bottle.

 Draw the mouth.

 Tie a scarf around the top or put a sock over the top for a hat.

 Have a parent cut a hole in the back for coins.

Family Fun Flying Disc Game

Emily and Cody love to spend time together as a family. They enjoy amusement park rides, but also enjoy fun times at home.

Here is Cody's favorite game. It's easy to play. All you need is a flying disc and a nice day outside.

Choose a starting place and then choose a target in your yard (a tree, the sandbox, a spot on the sidewalk.) The first player stands on the starting line and tries to hit the target. If the flying disc doesn't hit the target, the player goes to the spot where it landed and tries again from there. Count how many throws it takes to hit the target. After the first player hits the

target, the next player stands on the same starting line and tries to hit the same target.

Continue until everyone has had a turn. Then, go on to the next target. The player who has the lowest score after three targets wins!

In this chapter you read about how Mary and Joseph took care of Jesus. You learned how a mother polar bear prepares for the birth of her cubs and protects them, and you read about some ways that your parents take care of you. Hurry on to the next chapter for more crafts, games and fun!

☼ Chapter 5 ☼

My Siblings

Angelica dribbled the soccer ball past her younger brothers. She was just about ready to kick it in their homemade goal, when Raul came from behind and stole the ball. He passed it to Jose. Jose lifted it in the air with his toe and hit the ball with his head, passing it to Dylan. Dylan swiftly kicked it to James who nudged it into the goal. A point for the boys!

"Four against one. Something doesn't seem quite fair about this," Angelica said.

"You're bigger," James said. "It takes four of us to score against you."

Angelica laughed. "I'm not that good. Come on. Let's see if mom has the cookies ready yet."

The boys followed Angelica into the house. Sometimes her brothers

drove her crazy, but she was glad they were part of the family. After Angelica was born, her parents had decided to adopt children. Angelica hoped for a sister, but each time she'd gotten a brother. There were a lot of things

Angelica enjoyed doing with the boys like playing soccer or dodge ball, but Angelica secretly hoped that one day she would have a sister, too.

Bible Siblings

Martha   Mary   Lazarus

One day when Jesus was traveling, He came to the village of Bethany. There, Jesus visited the home of His three friends, , and . cleaned the house and made sure Jesus was comfortable. liked to cook and started to prepare a special meal for Jesus.

wanted to spend time listening to Jesus.

sat at His feet and listened to every word.

 was tired from getting everything ready.

thought that was being lazy. "Tell to help me

cook," said to Jesus.

Jesus told that had chosen to spend

time with Him and that was more important than

cooking.

On another day, when Jesus visited and ,

He found that had died. was very upset. "If

You had been here, would not have died,"

she said.

Jesus said that He would raise 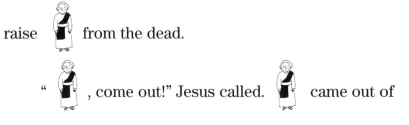 from the dead

so that people would see God's power and believe

that God had sent Him.

Jesus went to 🧍 ' tomb. He told the men to roll

back the stone. Then, Jesus prayed and asked God to

raise 🧍 from the dead.

" 🧍 , come out!" Jesus called. 🧍 came out of

the tomb. He was alive!

Mary, Martha, and Lazarus were siblings. The Bible

doesn't tell us about their childhood years, but they

probably played together and worked together while

they were growing up. When they became adults, they

loved Jesus and they loved each other.

Q: How did Martha feel about doing the work while Mary listened to Jesus?

_____

 Q: Why did Jesus raise Lazarus from the dead?

_____

Animal Friends

Animal Families: Pelican Chicks!

Do you ever compete with your brothers and sisters for attention, treats, privileges or other things? If so, you have sibling rivalry problems, just like pelicans do.

The mom and dad pelican build a nest together using twigs, grass, and feathers. The mom pelican often

lays two eggs at a time. The mom and dad take turns sitting on the eggs to keep them warm until they hatch. The first egg hatches a day ahead of the other egg. That gives the first chick a chance to start eating and growing before the other one is born. When the younger pelican arrives, the older one attacks it and tries to take all the food.

Perhaps you get annoyed at times because your older sibling takes the last cookie or gets the biggest piece of cake, but imagine what it would be like to be a pelican!

Sibling rivalry is when you compete — or even get into a fight — with brothers or sisters for attention. Maybe you compete over who gets to choose the movie to watch or over who has the most privileges. Can you think of a time this happened at your house?

Puzzle Pieces

Pelican Puzzle Verse

It's a good thing that you and your brothers and sisters don't treat each other like the pelican siblings do. If you do get upset with a sibling, here is a good verse to remember. Look at the word in each pelican bill. Write that word on the line with the matching number. *Puzzle answers appear at the back of the book.*

✷ Just for Me! ✷

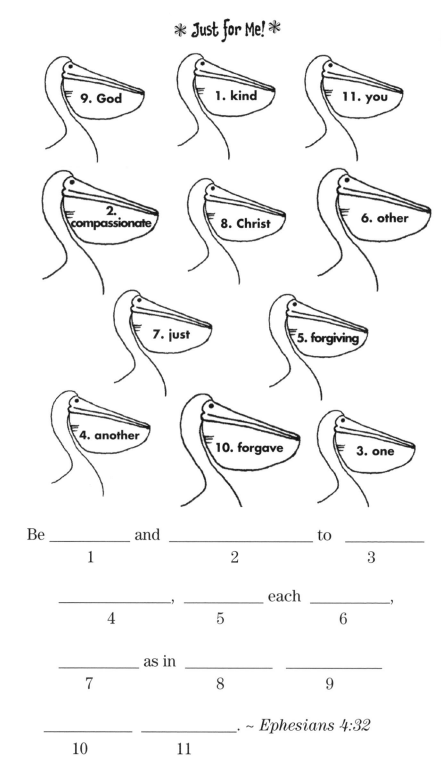

Be _____ and _____ to _____
       1   2   3

_____, _____ each _____,
      4   5   6

_____ as in _____ _____
      7   8   9

_____ _____. ~ *Ephesians 4:32*
    10   11

My Siblings

It might be hard to get along with siblings sometimes, but this verse tells us to be kind and compassionate to each other. If a sibling hurts your feelings or makes you angry, forgive him or her in the same way God forgives you.

What are two ways you can show kindness and compassion to your siblings today?

1. _____

_____

2. _____

_____

Brothers and Sisters Make Good Friends

Sometimes Angelica gets upset at her four younger brothers. She doesn't like it when they play in her room without permission or take one of her games or puzzles without asking her first. She didn't like it when Raul took her favorite ball outside and lost it in the big field behind their house. But most of the time they are all best friends.

✳ Just for Me! ✳

Angelica and her brothers are friends because:

1. They are close in age.

2. They like the same things.

3. They know how to fight fair.

4. They respect each other.

 They are Close in Age

Angelica and her brothers go to the same elementary school, except for James who isn't old enough for school yet. Dylan is in kindergarten, Jose and Raul are in first grade, and Angelica is in third grade. They walk to school and home again together. They tell each other about their day.

How old are your brothers or sisters? Write their names and ages below from youngest to oldest. Include yourself.

NAME: **AGE:**

♥ They Like the Same Things

Angelica and her brothers all like to play soccer, basketball, and baseball. They like to play games

outside. They don't like *all* the same things though. Angelica and Jose like to read, but Dylan, Raul, and James would rather watch television.

What things do you and your siblings like to do together?

_____

_____

What things do you like to do that they don't like to do?

_____

_____

♥ They Know How to Fight Fair

Like all siblings, Angelica and her brothers get into squabbles, but they do not hit or kick each other, say mean things, or damage each other's belongings. They listen to each other's side of the story. Then they try to work out the problem. That way no one is physically hurt and no one's feelings are hurt. If they aren't ready to talk about it, they go to their rooms to cool down first.

What is something that you fight about with a brother or sister? _____

How do you work it out?

_____

They Respect Each Other

Angelica and her brothers respect each other's belongings. Sometimes one of the boys takes something of Angelica's without asking and has to be reminded to

always ask first. They respect each other's privacy, too. They knock if the bathroom or bedroom doors are closed. They don't go in another person's bedroom without permission. They also respect each other's feelings. That is why they do not call names or say mean things.

Do you have a rule about name-calling? What is it?

_____

_____

Siblings Placemat

Here is a craft that you can do with your brothers and sisters. You can use these placemats each day at the dinner table.

 ## You Will Need:

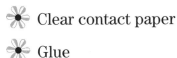 One large piece of construction paper for each person.

Photographs of each person or pictures cut out of a magazine of each person's favorite things such as dogs, horses, sports, etc.

Clear contact paper

Glue

 ## Do This:

❋ Each person should glue his or her pictures onto the construction paper. Allow the glue to dry.

❋ Have a parent cover both sides of the construction paper with clear contact paper. (You can also get the pages laminated at a copy shop.)

❋ Use your new placemats with your siblings the next time you have a meal together. If you spill food on your placemat, just wipe it off!

Outside Checkers Game

Angelica ran inside the house.

"Does anyone want to play checkers outside? I have the board already drawn."

"I do," Jose said. He grabbed the box of jar lids they used for playing pieces and followed her outside.

You can play checkers outside with a brother or sister, too.

You Will Need:

 Chalk

Twelve jar lids spray painted red or a favorite color.

Twelve jar lids spray painted black or a favorite color.

Do This:

 Draw a checkerboard on a large cement area, such as driveway, using chalk. Draw it eight squares wide and eight squares long.

Color in every other square with chalk. Be sure to start row one with a white square and the next row with a dark square.

Play just as you would on a regular checkerboard.

ou've read about Bible siblings who loved Jesus. You learned that pelicans have a real sibling rivalry problem. And you've learned some things that help you get along with your own brothers and sisters. Jump right into the next chapter for more ideas, fun, and activities!

My Extended Family

Samantha looked up from the book she was reading. "What does 'extended family' mean?" she asked her mom.

"Extended family?" Mom said as she sat down next to Samantha.

"Yes. In the story I am reading, a girl is going to spend Christmas with her extended family."

"That means she is going to spend it with people who are part of her family, but aren't her parents or brothers and sisters—people like grandparents, aunts, and uncles," Mom said.

"And her cousins?" Samantha shut her book and sat it beside her.

"Yes, her cousins, too."

"I'm glad Uncle Jim, Aunt Amber, and my cousins are coming to visit next week for spring break," Samantha said.

"I know you will have fun playing with Taylor, Victoria, and Sydney," Mom said.

"I can't wait," Samantha said twirling around. "I love my extended family."

"I'm glad," Mom said. "Family is important. Do you want to hear a story about a Bible family?'

"Yes," Samantha said sitting back down on the couch.

A Bible Family

Elimelech   Ruth   Naomi

King David   Two sons   Boaz

 , and their 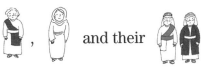 lived in Bethlehem

in the land of Judah. There was no food in Judah because

of a famine, so 's family traveled to the land of

Moab to live. The people in Judah worshipped the true

God but the people in Moab worshipped idols.

Not long after the family arrived in Moab, died.

The married two women from Moab named

 and Orpah. Years passed, and then the

died. Now , , and Orpah were all alone.

 knew the famine was

over in Judah and decided to return to Bethlehem.

 chose to leave her homeland and go with .

She told  ,

"Where you go I will go, and where you stay I will

stay. Your people will be my people and your God

will be my God."

Once the two women were back in Judah,

went into the barley field owned by and picked

up the grained that was always left behind for the poor.

 took care of herself and .

 saw what a kind person was to take

care of her mother-in-law. married . They

had a son named Obed. Obed was 's grandfather.

 Q: How did Ruth take care of Naomi?

Animal Families: Chimpanzee Family Groups!

Samantha was excited. Her aunt, uncle, and cousins were finally here for their visit. Today they were going to the zoo. This was one of Samantha's favorite places. She liked watching the lions and tigers, but they were usually asleep. She liked watching the

giraffes pull leaves off of trees with their silly long necks and tongues, too, but Samantha's favorite zoo animal is the chimpanzee.

A baby chimp is helpless when it is born. It stays with its mother many years to learn what it needs to know to survive on its own. A baby chimp is about seven years old when it leaves its mother.

Chimpanzees live in family groups made up of six to ten members. These family groups then join with other groups to form a community that may have up to 100 members. One or more male chimpanzees rule the community. They use body language, hand clapping, and facial expressions to communicate with the group.

Chimps, unlike monkeys, don't have tails. Chimps don't have hair on their face, hands or feet. They have large ears that help them hear other chimps in the forest.

How old is a chimp when it leaves its mother?

_____

How do chimps communicate?

_____

Getting Along

"Look at all the chimps," Samantha said to her cousins, Taylor, Victoria, and Sydney. "They all seem to get along so well."

"Not like us," Victoria said. "Sometimes we get into fights over the silliest stuff."

"Like who put the hairbrush in the wrong place or whose turn it is to pick what we watch on television," Sydney said.

"You wouldn't see chimps fighting over that kind of stuff," Taylor said.

"I guess they live out Romans 12:18," Aunt Amber said.

"What does that verse say?" Samantha asked.

"You will have to figure it out," Aunt Amber said.

Hidden Mirror Message

Can you figure it out? Hold the book up to a mirror to read the message. *Puzzle answers appear at the back of the book.*

Live at
peace
with everyone.
Romans 12:18

Extended Family

Do you have relatives who don't live with you—grandmas, grandpas, aunts, uncles, and cousins? Maybe they live in another city or state and they visit once in a while like Samantha's cousins. Or perhaps they live right in the same town as you and can visit frequently.

It's fun learning more about your extended family. You can ask your grandparents about their lives when they were your age. When they were born, personal computers were not yet invented and the internet was years away! They listened to records—not CDs or iPods. They wrote letters instead of e-mails.

Think of some questions you can ask your grandparents. You might ask them:

• What kind of school did you attend when you were in my grade?

• What was your favorite part of school when you were in my grade?

• Who was your best friend?

• What was your favorite thing to do with your friends?

• What was your favorite sport or hobby?

• Did you have a pet? What kind? What was its name?

�֎ Just for Me! �֎

Can you think of some more questions? Write them here:

_____

_____

_____

If your grandparents or other extended family members don't live close by, there are lots of fun ways to stay in touch. You can:

• Send pictures—you can either send prints by mail or digital photos by e-mail.

• Make a special scrapbook of pictures for them.

• Make a video of your life including activities such as your soccer game, helping your parents cook supper, singing in church choir, and whatever else is important to you.

• Make special birthday or Christmas cards for them.

• Send them a craft you make from this book.

What other ideas can you think of?

_____

_____

Family Book Project

Here is a project you can do to help you learn more about the family members you live with and your extended family. You can even do it together as a family. It doesn't matter if you were born or adopted into your family, or whether you live with your parents, an aunt and uncle, or your grandparents!

 ## You Will Need:

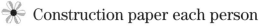

- Construction paper each person
- White paper
- Markers
- Glue
- Brads (fasteners) or stapler

 ## Do This:

Have an adult help you copy pages 97 and 98—one for each person you want to learn about.

❋ Fill out the page with help from your parents or the relative you're learning about if they live near you.

❋ Carefully cut out the page and glue it to a piece of colored construction paper. Attach a picture if you have one.

❋ Use one piece of construction paper to make a cover. Decorate as you like.

❋ After you have all the pages completed, carefully fasten the pages together with a stapler or with brads.

Name of family member

_____

Birthday _____

Place of birth _____

Name of school or college attended

_____

Favorite school memory

_____

Which sports did you play?

_____

Were you ever in the military?

_____

Did you live through any wars? What was that like?

_____

_____

_____

Who were your best friends?

_____

_____

What were your favorite hobbies?

_____

_____

What was your most important achievement?

_____

_____

_____

_____

_____

_____

_____

Other interesting facts or stories about the you

_____

_____

_____

_____

Write your own question here:

_____

_____

Answer:

_____

_____

_____

_____

Family Hide and Seek

After Samantha, Taylor, Victoria, and Sydney got home from the zoo, they decided to play a hide and seek game. It's easy and you can play it with your family. One person hides somewhere in the house while the others count to 50 or 100. Everyone goes in a different direction to search for the hidden family member. When a player finds the hidden family member, he or she hides with them. The last person to find the hidden group hides first the next time. Make sure to pick a big enough hiding place for everyone to fit!

In this chapter you learned that extended family members are relatives like aunts, uncles, cousins, and grandparents. You read about Ruth going to Naomi's homeland with her. You learned about Samantha's favorite zoo animal, the chimpanzee, and how chimpanzees live in family groups that make up a community. Keep reading! There are lots more ideas and activities ahead.

Chapter 7

Working Together

Rachel, Katie, and Gabriel were working in the garage. Their parents said they could have a garage sale if they worked together on it. They were going to send the money they made to an orphanage in Haiti to buy rice for the children to eat. Rachel was the oldest, so she was deciding what needed to be done.

Rachel found three large boxes in the garage. "First we need to decide what we are going to sell. We'll put those things into these boxes. Then, we'll put prices on each thing we're going to sell. Let's go to our rooms and see what we don't play with anymore."

Rachel found several stuffed animals she hadn't played with in a long time. Katie found some toy ponies and puzzles that she didn't need anymore. Gabriel still liked most of his toys and didn't want to part with any of them. Mom found some outgrown baby and toddler clothes for the sale.

Rachel, Katie, and Gabriel took the items and sorted them into the boxes—toys in one, stuffed animals in another, and clothes in the third. Dad and Mom were looking through storage boxes to see what could be sold. They found dishes, pans, and some tools they were willing to sell.

When they had gathered everything for the garage sale, Rachel and her parents put a price tag on each item. The next morning, they set up tables and put out the things for sale. Customers stopped by all day. Rachel and her parents collected the money.

"Wow, that was a lot of work," Rachel said when the last customer had pulled away.

"But it was worth it." Mom counted out the dollar bills and the coins.

"How much do we have for the orphanage?" Rachel asked.

"We have $311.00," Mom said.

"That's great," Rachel said. "That should buy lots of rice."

That night in her prayers, Rachel thanked God for the money for the orphanage. Then, her mother read her the story of Noah.

A Bible Family

Noah   Ark

God looked down at the world He had created

and was very sad. The people were not obeying Him.

They were not following His rules. Some people were

lying while others were stealing or cheating. Many

were worshipping false gods.

Only one man was living God's way. His name was

. God decided to destroy everyone but and

his family.

God warned that He was going to send a

flood to destroy the earth. God told to build an

 that would be 450 feet long, 75 feet wide, and

45 feet high. and his three sons cut and measured

boards. They fastened them together to build an

 just as God said. The women in 's family

worked by cooking and caring for their homes while

 and the three sons worked. It took 120 years

to build the (people lived much longer

back then.)

 's family worked together to do what God had

said. When the was finished, they gathered

the animals to go into the with them. When

they boarded, God shut the door and the rain began.

Soon, the whole world was under water, but and

his family were safe inside the they'd built.

 Q: What did God tell Noah to do?

_____

 Q: How did Noah's family work together?

_____

✳Animal Friends

Animal Families: Lion Prides!

Lions live in large groups called prides. A pride is made up of female lions—mothers, sisters, and cousins—along with their cubs and a few male lions that are not related to them. The lions in the pride are very close to each other. They will not normally let a stranger join.

Living together in a pride makes life easier. The females work together to raise the cubs and to hunt for food. They use teamwork when they hunt. Some lionesses chase the prey toward other lionesses who capture it. By working together, they can hunt bigger animals than they could if they hunted alone. The male lions hunt less than 10% of the time, but they patrol the territory and guard the cubs while the females hunt.

Because all the lions work together to feed and guard the pride, a cub born into a pride is twice as likely to survive as a cub born to a mother who is alone.

Why is a cub born into a pride more likely to survive than one that isn't?

_____

_____

How do the female lions work together?

_____

_____

Puzzle Pieces

Lion Puzzle Verse

Rachel, Katie, and Gabriel worked together to have a garage sale. A pride of lions works together to protect and provide food for each other. Working together and getting along with others, especially your family, is very important. How can you do this? The intsructions below will help.

The first clue in the verse shows **3** . Put one finger on the **3** and one finger on the 🦁. Bring your fingers together. You should be on the letter **O**. Write **O** on the first line. Continuing doing this until you can read the verse. *Puzzle answers appear at the back of the book.*

Working Together

And ____ ____ ____ ____ all
    3 🦁 4 🐾 1 🐾 3 🐾

____ ____ ____ ____ ____
4 🦁 2 🐾 1 🐾 3 🐾 1 🐾

virtues ____ ____ ____
    3 🐾 4 🐾 4 🦁

____ ____ love, which
3 🦁 2 🐾

____ ____ ____ ____ ____ them
1 🦁 2 🐾 2 🐾 1 🐾 3 🐾

all together ____ ____
    2 🐾 2 🐾

____ ____ ____ ____ ____ ____ ____
3 🐾 1 🐾 3 🐾 2 🦁 1 🐾 1 🐾 4 🦁

____ ____ ____ ____ ____.
4 🐾 2 🐾 2 🐾 4 🦁 4 🐾

~ Colossians 3:14

109

✳ Just for Me! ✳

Can you think of three ways to show love to someone in your family this week? List them below.

1.

2.

3.

Working Together

Rachel, Katie, and Gabriel knew how to work together. So did Noah and his family. Lion prides know how to work together, too. When you work together, you

are cooperating with each other. Being able to cooperate is an important skill to have both now while you are young, and later when you are an adult.

Cooperating means that no one gets his or her way all the time. Everyone helps and everyone gets a turn to choose.

110

Daily Jobs

If you don't have things that you do to help around the house, ask your parents to help you find one task to do each day. Write it on the chart below.

Day	Job
Sunday	
Monday	
Tuesday	
Wednesday	
Thursday	
Friday	
Saturday	

Make It!

Lion Pencil Topper

Here is a craft to remind you to work together just as the lions in a pride work together for food and protection.

 ## You Will Need:

 Orange craft foam

 Yellow craft foam

✳ Small black beads for eyes (or wiggle eyes)

✳ Small yellow beads for ears

✳ Glue

✳ Pipe cleaner

✳ Markers

▶ Do This:

✳ Trace the mane pattern onto the orange foam and cut out.

✳ Trace the face pattern onto the yellow foam and cut out.

✳ Glue the yellow face on top of the orange mane.

✳ Glue on the yellow beads for ears.

✳ Glue on the black beads for eyes.

✳ Draw on a nose and mouth. You can also draw on the eyes rather than use beads.

✳ Let the lion head dry.

✳ Tape or glue the pipe cleaner to the back of the lion's head.

Wrap the pipe cleaner around a pencil.

 Use your pencil to remind you to work together with others.

Lion patterns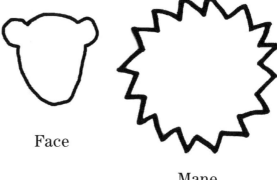

Face

Mane

"What is it" Game?

 You Will Need:

 Lots of small household items

 A paper sack

 Do This:

 Divide into two teams of two. If some players are very young, you can add them to a team that already has two players.

✳ The first team finds three small objects from around the house and puts them in the bag.

✳ They give the closed bag to one of the players on the other team.

✳ That player puts their hand in the bag and grabs one object. Without looking or taking the object out of the bag, the player must describe it to their partner using only three clues.

✳ The partner must guess what the object is.

✳ After all three objects are described, the second team takes the bag and fills it with three objects.

✳ The team that first successfully guesses ten items wins the game.

✳ You have to play as a team to win!

Chapter 8

Playing Together

✳ Just for Me! ✳

Chloe, Nicholas, and David were at the marine park. Their grandparents had taken them because it was Chloe's birthday and this was her favorite place for special occasions. Chloe liked looking at the small fish in the aquariums. There were all sorts of brightly colored fish swimming together.

After they watched the fish for a while, it was time for the sea lion show. Chloe, Nicholas and David clapped and laughed at the funny animal performers in the show.

Chloe couldn't believe how well trained the sea lions were. She wondered if she should be a marine biologist and learn how to train sea animals.

After the sea lion show, they went to the whale performance. Chloe watched as the large black and white animals swam in the big tank of water. The crowd cheered as three trainers dove into the water and then came up riding on the backs of the whales.

After the whole show ended, they all hurried to the stadium for Chloe's favorite event — the dolphin show.

The seats were filling up quickly. Everyone loved the dolphin show. Chloe borrowed Grandpa's camera and took pictures as the dolphins jumped and played in the water. She got a picture of the trainer diving off the nose of a dolphin.

Chloe was sad when it was time to go home. She couldn't wait until they visited the marine park again. On the way home, Grandma told the kids stories about children in the Bible.

Jesus' Family

Children   Girls   Boys

Many people are familiar with the story of Jesus'

birth. However, the Bible tells us very little about His life

from His birth until He was twelve years old.

Did Jesus and other   in Bible times play? Of

course they did. But they didn't have many toys. They

played with sticks and string or broken pottery. Richer

117

✻ Just for Me! ✻

may have had clay dolls that they dressed in scraps

of cloth. The   probably played together outside.

They may have run races and made up games just as you

do with your friends. The   went to school where

they learned to read and write.   didn't go to school.

They stayed home and learned how to cook and clean.

Even though times were very different then, the

loved to talk and play with their families and

friends just as you do today.

Q: What is your favorite game to play?

_____

Q: What do you think Jesus might have

liked to play? _____

*Animal Friends

Animal Families: Dolphin Schools!

Chloe, Nicholas, and David enjoyed the dolphin show. They laughed and clapped all the way through it. Chloe loves dolphins because they are such playful animals. During the show they tossed balls to each other with their noses, jumped through hoops, and appeared to dance across the top of the water. The trainer told the crowd that dolphins are made for swimming. They have long, slender snouts, smooth skin, flippers, and dorsal fins. They have a streamlined body that allows water to roll right over their bodies. A baby dolphin is called a calf.

Dolphins are very agile. They can swim fast and leap into the air. That makes them fun to watch. In the open water, they swim in groups called schools. The school may have as few as five

dolphins or as many as a hundred or more. They may leap out of the water in front of a boat's bow or play in the wake of the boat. When a dolphin is sick, hurt, or having a baby, all the dolphins help protect it. Dolphins play together and they take care of each other, too.

Why does Chloe like dolphins the best?

_____

What other animals have you seen that are playful?

_____

Dolphin Puzzle Verse

God wants us to be happy. Match the numbers on the lines below with the numbers on the dolphins to read the verse. *Puzzle answers appear at the back of the book.*

_____ the _____ be _____ and
　　1　　　　　　　2　　　　　　　3

_____ before _____ ;
　　4　　　　　　　5

may _____ be _____ and
　　　6　　　　　　　7

_____ . ~ *Psalm 68:3*
　8

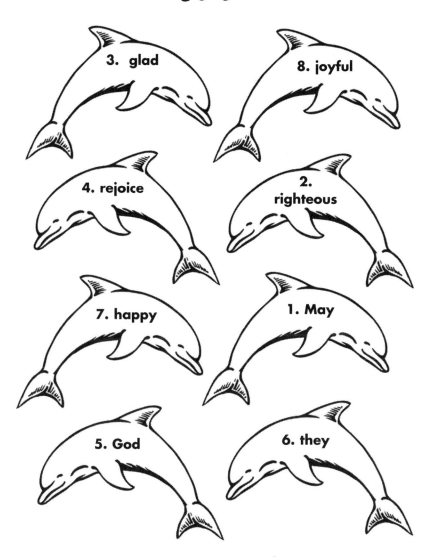

3. glad

8. joyful

4. rejoice

2. righteous

7. happy

1. May

5. God

6. they

Family Fun Book

You can keep track of your favorite family activities by making a family fun book.

121

You Will Need:

 A spiral notebook

 Crayons or markers

 Pictures of your favorite activities either cut from a magazine or taken on your camera and printed out

 Glue

Scissors

 ## Do This:

 Decorate the front of your notebook with the words "ABCs of Fun." Use crayons or markers or cut the letters from a magazine and glue them on.

✳ Write a letter of the alphabet on each page. Letter A would be on the first page, B on the second page, and so on. You may want to just use the fronts of pages.

✳ Find a picture of a favorite activity that starts with each letter.

✳ Write the name of the activity and glue the picture on each page. For example, you might write "Animal charades" on the first page and glue pictures of animals on that page. You might write "Balloon relay" on the next page and add a picture of a balloon or of your family playing balloon relay.

 Use the book to remind you of your favorite activities or to help you think of something to do when you are bored.

Soak Them Tag

After Chloe got home from the marine park, she played a game with Nicholas and David. This is their favorite game to play in warm weather. You can play it, too.

 You Will Need:

 Large, soft sponge
 Bucket of water

 Do This:

 Select one person to be IT.

 The person who is IT drops the sponge into the bucket of water to get it wet.

123

✱ Everyone else runs away.

✱ IT tries to tag the players by throwing the wet sponge at them.

✱ When someone is tagged, that person becomes IT.

✱ You won't have to argue about whether the players were hit or not because you will see a wet spot on their back if they were hit!

In this chapter you've read about Chloe, Nicholas, and David at the marine park. You read about how playful dolphins are and how they take care of each other. You've also learned some ways you can have fun with your family. There's more ahead, Keep going!

Chapter 9

Serving Together

Destiny pulled on her coat and followed her parents to the car. They drove to their church and went inside to the big area that was used for serving meals. Every month, their church prepared a meal for all the homeless and poor people in their community. The church then showed a movie following the meal.

Destiny and her parents helped with the meals. This was their fourth time helping. She and her dad set out plates and silverware. Her mom stirred a big pot of mashed potatoes.

"I'm glad we are helping with the meal," Destiny said to her dad. "I was afraid at first, but now that I know the people, I'm not. It's sad when the children

come in hungry. I can't imagine what it would be like to not have our home or food to eat."

Dad set a large pile of plates next to the serving line. "God has blessed our family. Helping tonight is one way of thanking Him. It also reminds us to be grateful for what we have."

After the meal, Destiny helped wipe the tables and

clean the dining area. Later that night, Destiny got ready for bed. "Can you read me a Bible story?" she asked her dad.

"Yes, I will read you a story about a family who served God together." Her dad pulled a big Bible storybook from the shelf.

A Family Serves God

Zechariah   Elizabeth   John

Temple   Angel

and believed in God. They followed

God's commandments. They prayed and worshipped

God. was a priest. He participated in all of the

duties that priests performed.

127

One day, it was 's turn to burn incense. This

was part of Hebrew worship. A priest would go into the

 and burn the incense before God. Then, he

would come out and give a blessing to the people.

When went into the 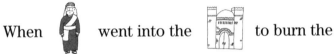 to burn the

incense, an angel appeared and spoke to him. The

 told that God would give him a son.

 asked the how this could be because

he and his wife were too old to have a child.

The told that since he had not

believed, he would not be able to speak until the baby

was born. When came out of the , he

couldn't give the people a blessing because he wasn't

able to talk. made signs to them, and they knew

he had seen a vision in the .

 and had a baby boy just as the

 said. The people thought he would be named

after , but told them that the baby's name

would be John.

 wrote "His name is John." Then, was

able to speak again.

As grew up, he served God by getting people

ready for Jesus' message. told the people about

God and about One "whose sandals I am not worthy to

untie." told the people that they needed to be

forgiven of their sins.

Jesus came to to be baptized. After Jesus was

baptized, a dove descended on Him and a voice from

Heaven said, "You are my Son, whom I love; with you I

am well pleased" (Luke 3:22).

 , and all loved and served God.

 Q: How did Elizabeth serve God?

Q: How did Zechariah serve God?

_____

 Q: How did John serve God?

_____

*Animal Friends

Animal Families: Giraffe Calves!

Giraffes are very tall animals. They could look right into one of your upstairs windows with no problem. A giraffe's neck is six feet long and the neck weighs 600 pounds all by itself. A giraffe's legs are also six feet long.

Giraffes need a lot of food to keep their tall bodies running. Giraffes may eat 75 pounds of food a day—that is probably more than you weigh! Their tongues are 18″ long and help

them get food from trees and other places. How long do you think your tongue is?

A baby giraffe is called a calf. When a calf is born, it drops six feet to the ground! This causes it to take a big breath of air, but the calf does not get hurt. After about an hour, the calf gets up and walks.

One mother giraffe stays with all the calves while the others go out to find food to eat. The "babysitter" giraffe keeps the calves safe until the other mothers are home again. They work together so that everyone gets to eat.

How do giraffes help each other?

_____

The Key to Serving

Destiny and her family serve at their church. Zechariah served God in the temple. Giraffe mothers serve other giraffe mothers by "babysitting" their calves. What does the Bible say about serving? Look at the two letters below each line. Write the letter that comes between them on the line. *Puzzle answers appear at the back of the book.*

___ ___ ___ ___ ___   ___ ___ ___

rt   df   qs   uw   df   np   mo   df

___ ___ ___ ___ ___ ___ ___

zb   mo   np   su   gi   df   qs

___ ___ ___   ___ ___ ___ ___.

hj   mo   km   np   uw   df

~ Galatians 5:13

What does this verse say is the key to serving?

_____

_____

Make It!

Gift Boxes

Destiny and her parents like helping with the monthly meal at the church, but that is not all they do. They also make gift boxes for babies and take them to the pregnancy center. Destiny and her parents get a big box, wrap it in baby paper, and fill it up with things a baby might need. Destiny loves to go shopping with her parents to buy things for the baby boxes. They buy diapers, bottles,

sleepers, and a baby toy. Then they take it to the pregnancy center for someone who

really needs it. Destiny knows that when her family does this, they are serving others in love.

Your family can make a box for someone, too. Your gift box may be for someone in the military, an elderly person in a nursing home who is lonely, a young mother, or a sick child. Discuss this with your whole family. You may want to make more than one box.

 You Will Need:

 A shoebox

 Colorful wrapping paper

 Items for the gift box

Do This:

 Go to the store and pick out several items to go into the gift box. Choose things that person will like or need.

 Wrap your shoebox in wrapping paper. Wrap the lid separately so it can be taken off and put back on without ruining the paper.

Fill the box with the items you bought.

Deliver or mail the box.

People Pancakes

Want to do something nice for your family? Have an adult help you make this breakfast treat.

You Will Need:

 Pancake batter

 Griddle

 Use fruit for eyes, nose, and mouth. Strawberries, blueberries, and banana slices work well.

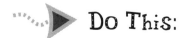

Do This:

❀ Have a parent help you make the pancake batter.

❀ Decorate the pancakes by making faces with the fruit.

❀ Serve them to your family members.

In this chapter you read how Destiny and her family serve others. You read about a Bible family who served God and about how giraffes help each other. **You also learned several ways that you can serve others!** Be sure to read on—there's still more fun ahead.

❀ Chapter 10 ❀

Special Times

Olivia bounced up and down. "Is it time to go yet?" she asked. Olivia and her younger brother, Austin, were getting ready to go to the parade. Their older siblings were in the marching bands that would be playing in the parade.

Mom, Dad, Olivia, and Austin walked a few blocks to their local parade and found a great spot from which to view the parade. When the police cars at the front of the parade turned on their sirens, Austin put his hands over his ears. He didn't like loud noises. A few minutes later they could hear a band.

"It's the middle school band. Look for Nathan and Jonathan," Olivia told Austin. They watched for their brothers who played trombones in the middle school

band. Dad put Austin on his shoulders so he could see better. He waved to his brothers.

After the band passed by, little cars drove in circles up and down the street. Suddenly, Olivia heard the high school band. She looked for her sister, Anna, who played drums. She waved as Anna went by even though she knew her sister couldn't see her.

The final parade participants were rodeo riders on horseback followed by a fire truck. Oliva was sad—she loved parades and wished there was one every week.

On their walk back home, Mom and Dad told the kids about a great celebration in the Bible.

Miriam's Celebration

Miriam   Moses   Baby Moses

 was ' older sister. One day

 's mother sent her to sit watch over her brother

 who was hidden in a basket in the reeds along

the river. His family hid him there to keep him safe from

the evil ruler who wanted to harm all the baby boys.

✳ Just for Me! ✳

One day the Pharaoh's daughter was bathing in the

river and found . She decided to keep him but

she needed someone to care for the baby until he was

old enough to live in the palace with her. ran to

get her mother who was then hired to care for

until he was old enough to live at the palace.

Later became a prophetess and a leader in the

Hebrew community. A prophetess encouraged the

people to love and obey God. proclaimed

God's truth.

One day led the Israelite slaves out of the

land of Egypt. The Pharaoh and his men chased the

Israelites in their chariots. They didn't want to lose their

slaves. They wouldn't have anyone to do their work for them.

Soon, the Israelites were at the Red Sea with

nowhere to go. When they saw the soldiers coming after

them, they were afraid. They called out to to

do something.

 said, "Do not be afraid. Stand firm and you

will see the deliverance God will bring you today."

 raised his rod over the Red Sea. The waters

divided and there was a dry path right through the

middle of the sea! It took a long time for all the

thousands and thousands of Israelites to cross the Red

Sea. God held the water back until the last Israelite was

safely across. As the Egyptians approached, God let the

mighty waters flow back and He swept the Egyptians

into the sea. The entire army was destroyed.

 sang a song to the Lord. "I will sing to the

Lord for he is highly exalted. The horse and his rider he

has hurled into the sea."

 took a tambourine and led the women in

singing and dancing. She sang, "Sing to the Lord, for he

is highly exalted. The horse and its rider he has hurled

into the sea." sang and danced in praise to God. It

was a time for celebration. God had delivered His

people. *(Exodus 15)*

Q: How do you think the people felt when they saw the Egyptians swept into the sea?

_____

_____

 Q: Why was Miriam celebrating?

_____

*Animal Friends

Animal Families: Monkey Troups!

Monkeys may not have celebrations like the one Miriam led, but they do like to have fun. Monkeys live in groups called troups. Monkey troups travel together to find food. Baby monkeys who are too small to walk on their own ride on their mother's backs instead.

Monkeys are very social animals. They use sounds, expressions, and body movements to communicate. If you see a monkey that seems to be smiling, it's actually a sign of aggression or anger. Monkeys express affection or make

peace by grooming each other. Grooming also helps keep their fur free from dirt and bugs.

When troups are not traveling, the babies are very playful. They are active most of their waking hours. Playing helps the babies build up the physical and social skills that they need for adult life. It also makes them fun to watch.

How do baby monkeys travel?

_____

How do monkeys communicate?

_____

Puzzle Pieces

Balloon Puzzle Verse

Olivia loves celebrations. That's why she likes parades and why she likes the story of Miriam. Her favorite book of the Bible is Psalms. Many of the psalms are written as praises to God. Fill in the missing words in Olivia's favorite psalm. To solve this puzzle, find the number in the balloon that matches the number under each blank line. Write the word from the balloon in that space. *Puzzle answers appear at the back of the book.*

Special Times

_____ for joy to the _____, all the earth.
1 2

_____ the LORD with _____;
3 4

come before him with _____ _____.
5 6

~ Psalm 100:1-2

Piñata

The next time you have a family celebration, you can make a piñata to add to the fun. It takes time to dry and decorate so start several days ahead.

 You Will Need:

 Flour

 Water

 Two bowls—one for mixing papier mache and one for holding the balloon while you work

 Spoon

 Salt

 Large heart shaped balloon

Tissue paper in your favorite color

Newspaper

Glue

 Heavy string or twine

 # Do This:

First, make the papier mache:

* Mix 1½ cups of flour with two cups of water.
* Mix until you get a thick paste.
* Add more water or flour until the mixture is the consistency of thick glue.
* Add two tablespoons of salt.

Then, make the piñata:

* Inflate the balloon.
* Balance the balloon in the bowl to support it while you work. You will have to turn it as you make the piñata.
* Tear the newspaper pages into 1½ inch strips.
* Drag a piece of the newspaper through the papier mache mixture.

* Run your fingers down the strips to get off any extra papier mache.

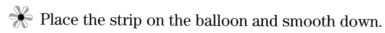
❋ Just for Me! ❋

❋ Place the strip on the balloon and smooth down.

❋ Continue doing the same thing with the strips of paper, overlapping the strips on the balloon until the whole balloon is covered in one layer of paper. Smooth carefully after each strip.

❋ Leave a two-inch opening at the top of the piñata in order to fill it with candy and treats.

❋ Allow the piñata to dry. (Cover any left over papier mache with plastic wrap.)

❋ Do a second layer of paper strips and papier mache. You may even need a third coat.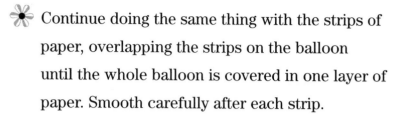

❋ Pop the balloon and allow the piñata to dry again.

❋ Cut the tissue paper into two inch squares.

❋ Coat the tissue paper squares with glue and stick them to the piñata just as you did the paper strips by overlapping each piece.

❋ Cover the piñata with one or two layers of tissue paper.

❋ Allow the piñata to dry.

❋ Fill the dry piñata with candy and other small treats.

❋ Cover the opening with tissue paper.

❋ Punch two holes near the top of the piñata.

Run the twine through the holes and use it to hang the piñata. If the piñata is very heavy, you may want to punch four holes and use two separate pieces of string to hang it.

Praise Celebration

You can praise God with instruments like Miriam did. Put on a praise CD and invite your family and friends to praise God with you! You can even make a very simple plastic egg shaker for everyone!

 You Will Need:

 Plastic Easter eggs

Rice

Glue

Empty egg carton

Paint, markers, or stickers

 **Do This:**

✽ Put one tablespoon of rice into the bottom of the egg.

✽ Put a strip of glue around the open edge of the top of the egg.

✽ Push the halves together and let them dry.

✽ Apply stickers to the egg.

✽ Decorate the egg carton and use it to store your egg shakers.

In this chapter, you learned how to have special times of celebration with your family. Is there a holiday coming up or a special day that you can celebrate? Talk to your parents and make some fun plans for the day. And most of all, enjoy being a family!

Chapter 1

Family Puzzle Verse

God sets the lonely in families. Psalm 68:6

Chapter 2

Penquin Puzzle Verse

Let love and faithfulness never leave you; bind them around your neck, write them on the tablet of your heart. Proverbs 3:3.

Chapter 3

Care About Each Other Kite Puzzle Verse

Therefore, as God's chosen people, holy and dearly loved, clothe yourselves with compassion, kindness, humility, gentleness and patience. Bear with each other and forgive whatever grievances you may have against one another. Forgive as the Lord forgave you.

Colassians 3:12-13

Chapter 4

Parent Puzzle Verse

Children, obey your parents in the Lord, for this is right.

Ephesians 6:1

Chapter 5

Pelican Puzzle Verse

Be kind and compassionate to one another, forgiving each other, just as in Christ God forgave you. Ephesians 4:32

Chapter 6

Hidden Mirror Message

*Live at peace with
everyone.* Romans 12:18

Chapter 7

Lion Puzzle Verse

*And over all these virues put on love, which binds them all
together in perfect unity.* Colossians 3:14

Chapter 8

Dolphin Puzzle Verse

*May the righteous be glad and rejoice before God; may they
be happy and joyful.* Psalm 68:3

Chapter 9

The Key to Serving

Serve one another in love. Galatians 5:13

Chapter 10

Balloon Puzzle Verse

*Shout for joy to the Lord, all the earth. Worship the Lord with
gladness; come before him with joyful songs.* Psalm 100:1-2